Cain & Abel
Finding the Fruits of Peace

by Sandy Eisenberg Sasso
Illustrated by Joani Keller Rothenberg

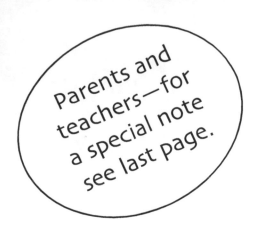
Parents and teachers—for a special note see last page.

For Floyd,
My Brother, My Friend,
with Love—S.E.S.

For My Children,
Leela, Ben Tamir, Maya, and Tal—J.K.R.

Cain & Abel: Finding the Fruits of Peace
2007 Second Printing

Library of Congress Cataloging-in-Publication Data
Sasso, Sandy Eisenberg.
Cain and Abel : finding the fruits of peace / by Sandy Eisenberg Sasso ; illustrated by Joani Keller Rothenberg.
    p. cm.
Summary: Retells the story of two brothers who, after years of sharing everything, become angry enough to lose control and bring violence into the world.
ISBN-13: 978-1-58023-123-7 (hc.)
ISBN-13: 978-1-68336-688-1 (pbk.)
1. Cain (Biblical figure)—Legends. 2. Abel (Biblical figure)—Legends. 3. Bible. O.T. Genesis IV, 1–16—Criticism, interpretation, etc., Jewish—Juvenile literature. 4. Midrash—Juvenile literature. 5. Anger—Juvenile literature. [1. Cain (Biblical figure) 2. Abel (Biblical figure) 3. Midrash. 4. Anger.] I. Rothenberg, Joani Keller, 1964– ill. II. Title.
BS580.C3 S27 2001
222'.1109505—dc21

2001002206

Book and jacket design: Drena Fagen

For People of All Faiths, All Backgrounds
Published by Jewish Lights Publishing
www.jewishlights.com

In the beginning God created each tree so that it could yield many different kinds of fruit. Then Cain killed his brother, Abel, and the trees went into mourning. From then on each tree would yield just one kind of fruit. Only in the world to come will the trees return to their full fruitfulness.

—from *Midrash Tanhuma*

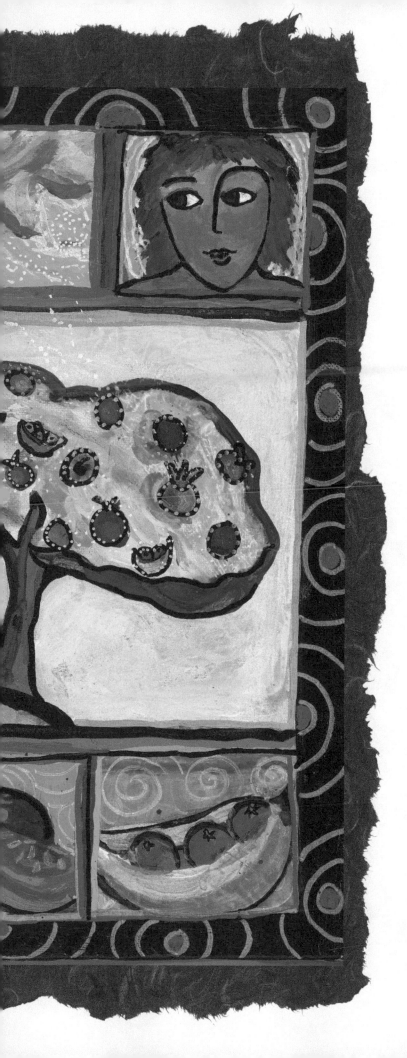

A very long time ago, when the world was new, many different kinds of fruit grew on each and every tree. Orapples, plumelons, and banangerines ripened on a single branch. The smell of pinango, limeberry, and waterloupe sweetened the air.

Two children walked in God's garden called Earth. One was named Cain, the other, Abel. They were the first children, the first brothers.

Cain and Abel loved the taste of orapples, plumelons, and banangerines. They loved the smell of pinango, limeberry, and waterloupe. The earth was warm and soft, and fruit trees grew in abundance.

Each brother had a special job.

Cain was the farmer. He loved to dig in the earth and harvest the vegetables and fruits. He knew how to take the wheat of the field, grind it into flour, and bake bread.

Abel was the shepherd. He liked to watch as his sheep grazed in the fields, and he gently guided the strays back to the flock. He would shear their wool and spin it into soft yarn to make blankets.

Cain's hair was straight and coarse like straw from the grain he planted. Abel's hair was soft and curly like the wool on the sheep he tended. Cain noticed that when he was alongside his brother, Abel reached only to his chin. Abel saw how large Cain's hands were compared to his own.

But when they stood face to face, they saw that their eyes were the same color of chestnut. Every spring Cain and Abel marveled at the birth of lambs and the ripening of wheat.

In the cool of the evening, Cain wrapped himself in Abel's wool and Abel dined on Cain's vegetable stew. Late at night, wrapped in soft blankets and feasting on sweet plumelons, the brothers told each other their dreams.

One day Cain and Abel argued about whether it was better to be a farmer or a shepherd. Cain insisted that God loved the farmer best.

"After all, God planted the first garden," he declared.

Abel argued that God loved the shepherd best. "After all, God created the animals and watches over them," he insisted.

Cain and Abel prayed to God. When Cain prayed, he brought with him a large basket of ripened vegetables. When Abel prayed, he brought his very finest sheep.

Cain looked at his silent vegetables, shriveling up in the noon sun while Abel's sheep bleated happily in the field. Cain was certain that God must like sheep better than vegetables. Maybe God *did* like the shepherd better than the farmer.

Cain glared at his brother. That night he didn't cover himself with Abel's blanket, and he didn't tell Abel his dreams. The next day he didn't share his vegetable stew with Abel. Abel did not understand why Cain was so angry at him.

At night, Cain thought about how everything seemed so easy for Abel. If it weren't for his brother, *he* would be the favorite one. If it weren't for Abel, he'd be happy. Just thinking about it made Cain's face turn red like the beets he grew.

"I hate you, Abel!" he called out.

Hearing Cain's words, Abel turned pale like sheep's wool.

"I hate you too, Cain!" Abel shouted.

From then on, whenever Cain and Abel met in the field, they turned their faces away from each other. For weeks they could not look each other in the eye.

One hot morning Cain was clearing some heavy rocks from the ground. A sheep from Abel's flock trampled on Cain's newly planted field. Abel was lying in the shade of a nearby tree while his sheep grazed lazily. Cain tried to speak to Abel, but the words wouldn't come.

Cain hated that his brother was resting while the sheep made a mess of all his hard work. Cain was so angry that he felt as if he were on fire inside. His heart was beating so strongly that he covered his ears to make the pounding stop, but it just got louder. He couldn't even look at Abel anymore; he could only stare at the ground.

At that moment, Cain noticed a large rock sitting right by his feet. Without thinking, he lifted the rock and instead of tossing it aside as he always did, he threw it at Abel and hit him on the head.

Abel fell over and did not move. Cain called to him, but Abel did not answer. It was then that Cain knew he had killed his brother, Abel.

Cain wanted to run away, but his feet would not carry him and his hands trembled. The sky darkened.

Then Cain heard God's voice calling to him, "Where is your brother?"

God's voice was angry and sad.

Cain answered, "Am I my brother's keeper?"

The rock that seemed so light a moment ago was heavy in Cain's heart. The gash in Abel's head appeared as a mark on Cain's own.

Cain wished he could go back in time and take back his anger, take back the rock. He missed his brother; he felt ashamed. Abel would never grow up and have children.

It was as if Cain had destroyed an entire world.

The earth that had always felt warm and soft beneath his feet turned cold and hard. Where once fruits and flowers bloomed, now only thorns and thistles grew. Cain couldn't farm anymore. He wandered from place to place looking for a home.

Winter came early that year and the trees wept leaves. All kinds of fruit fell before they ripened. Figterines, rasdew, and cantaberry covered the ground. No longer could different kinds of fruit remain on a single tree.

Time passed, a long time.
The world was not new anymore.
People built cities and made homes
there. Yet people often spoke angry
words. And with angry words they
drew their swords. Swords turned to
guns and guns to bombs.

One killing became two, two became
four, and four became sixteen.
Sixteen killings became war.

Entire worlds were destroyed.

Now no one remembers figterines, rasdew, and cantaberry. But the people keep telling the story of Cain and Abel, the first children. They sigh as they read of Cain picking up the rock. They want to hold back his hand and stop his anger from growing into hate.

Perhaps one day, when each person learns to reach out an open hand without the rock, without the sword, without the gun, the entire world can be saved.

Then many different kinds of fruit will once again grow
on a single tree. The orapples will return, the banangerines will appear.
And in God's garden called Earth, all will be good.

A Special Note to Parents and Teachers

The story of Cain and Abel is an ancient tale that is all too modern. Every day our children see what happens when anger goes awry. As much as we might wish, we cannot shield them from the fighting that exists on the playground, in school, on television, and in video games. We need more than ever to talk with our youngsters about what makes the natural emotion of anger erupt into violence.

Cain and Abel's story offers us an opportunity to discuss with our children positive ways of dealing with the common feelings of hurt, jealousy, and rejection. With this story, we—together with our sons and daughters—can imagine what the world would be like without violence. Imagining it just might be the beginning of making it so.

Some Questions for Adults and Kids to Explore Together:

- I wonder if you ever feel like Cain?

- What might Cain and Abel have said to each other to have made things different?

- Think of times when you are angry. What makes you feel this way?

- How do you act when you are angry? Do you ever wish you could act differently?

- Imagine you are one of the trees in the story. What are you feeling? What might you say to the other trees? To Cain?

- What can you do to bring back the many different kinds of fruit?

Printed in the USA
CPSIA information can be obtained
at www.ICGtesting.com
JSHW072027140824
68134JS00043B/3820

9 781683 366881